In a close-kn
little boy na
handicap big brother, Javar. Jade admired
Javar so much; he was his superhero. They
were always together, and Javar helped Jade
even though he was in a wheelchair.
MW01644760

Together, they helped each other. Javar helped Jade with homework and Jade helped take care of Javar feeding him. At night time Javar told Jade stories of him wanting to help people in his community if he only wasn't in a wheelchair

This Book Belongs To

____

____

____

But one fateful day, a
terrible event unfolded -
Javar went to heaven.

Jade was heartbroken and missed his big brother more than words could express.

Every night, Jade looked at a
photo of Javar, reminiscing
about their adventures.

To honor Javar's memory, they decided to plant a tree together, symbolizing his strength and resilience.

Jade remembered Javar's spirit of helping others and started assisting his friends at school.

On clear nights, Jade would look at the stars, feeling as though Javar was watching over him.

As time went on, Jade made new friends
who helped him heal and smile once more.

Together with his mom, Jade continued Javar's legacy by doing acts of kindness within their community.

Jade still thought about Javar every day, knowing his big brother's love would always be a part of him.

The tree they planted for Javar grew strong, just like the love in Jade's heart.

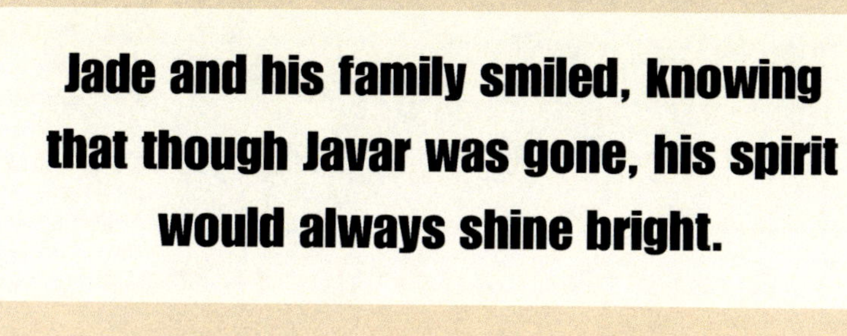

Jade and his family smiled, knowing that though Javar was gone, his spirit would always shine bright.

Dedication Page

For all the little hearts that carry big emotions, This book is dedicated to the brave and resilient kids navigating the journey of grief. To those who, like our main character Jade, have faced the challenge of saying goodbye to a superhero sibling, this story is for you. To the families who support, comfort, and cherish these young hearts, offering solace and understanding in moments of sorrow, your strength and love shine brightly. May the pages of this book serve as a gentle reminder that love transcends time and space, and our cherished memories become the guiding stars in our darkest nights. In honor of every superhero sibling turned guardian angel, this story is a testament to the enduring power of love. With heartfelt empathy and a deep understanding of the unique journey you're on,

Jade’s Mom

Resource Page:

"My Superhero Brother Is Now My Angel" Grief Support Organizations: GriefShare: (https://www.griefshare.org/)

The Dougy Center for Grieving Children & Families: (https://www.dougy.org/)

National Alliance for Grieving Children (NAGC): (https://childrengrieve.org/)

Counseling and Therapeutic Resources: Find a Therapist: (https://www.psychologytoday.com/us/therapists)

Online Communities for Families Coping with Loss: (https://grieving.com/)

What's Your Grief (https://whatsyourgrief.com/community/)

Memorialization Ideas: Creating Memory Journals: Memory Journal Guide (https://www.goodtherapy.org/blog/how-to-createa-grief-journal-0118185)

Planting a Memorial Tree or Garden: Ideas for Memorial Gardens (https://www.familyhandyman.com/project/memorial-garden/)

Resource Page (Continued):

School and Community Support: - Talking to Teachers and School Counselors: National Association of School Psychologists - Resources (https://www.nasponline.org/resourcesand-publications/resources-and-podcasts)

Child-Friendly Resources: Sesame Street in Communities - Grief: Sesame Street in Communities - Grief (https://sesamestreetincommunities.org/topics/grief/)

Local Resources for Black Kids in New Jersey: New Jersey Black Therapists Network: (https://www.njbtn.org/)

Resource Page (Continued):

African American Mental Health Providers:
Directory - Psychology Today
(https://www.psychologytoday.com/us/therapists/african-american)

Remember: You are not alone in this journey. Seek support, embrace memories, and allow healing to take its course.

If you need immediate assistance, consider reaching out to a mental health professional or a local crisis hotline.

Made in the USA
Middletown, DE
22 April 2024

53241812R00015